ELTON JOHN
IN CONVERSATION WITH
ANDY PEEBLES
'21 at 33'

BRITISH BROADCASTING CORPORATION

In the same series
THE LENNON TAPES

Published by the
British Broadcasting Corporation
35 Marylebone High Street
London W1M 4AA

ISBN 0 563 17981 3

First published 1981

Printed and bound in England by
Jolly & Barber Ltd, Rugby

CONTENTS

FOREWORD

To commemorate the truly gargantuan output of having released twenty-one million selling albums by the time he had reached the age of thirty-three, we thought it would be a worthwhile idea for Radio One to ask Elton to do an 'in depth' programme for us, which mirrored chronologically both his career and music.

Both Andy Peebles and myself have had connections with Elton over the years – some of Elton's very first radio sessions were for my shows on Radio One – and in 1979 Andy went to Moscow to present Elton's now historic first 'live' concert from Russia for Radio One.

Elton John, having agreed to my idea, suggested that we came down and actually recorded the interview at his house, 'way down' in the Berkshire countryside.

At around six p.m. on a hot July evening, we arrived outside the portals of Elton's truly magnificent home; after some stringent security checks the electric gates lifted and we made our way up the drive to Elton's front door. Elton was in an ebullient and friendly mood, warmly greeting us and taking us almost immediately to see his amazingly large record collection and private discotheque.

The BBC Outside Broadcast recording unit was already set up in Elton's drawing room – complete with his Steinway, with cables running through to his study where the actual interview would take place. After some level checks, the tapes were set in motion and the conversation just went on and on for almost three hours!

Elton, himself a natural raconteur, provided us in this

interview with a most valuable insight into his personality and music, the result being first transmitted on Radio One on August Bank Holiday Monday 1980. This book, *The Elton John Tapes*, is a transcription of the Andy Peebles Radio One interview with Elton.

PAUL WILLIAMS
Senior Producer Radio One

INTRODUCTION

Although I had long admired the man's music, my first encounter with EJ 'in person' was in 1975 when he guested on my radio show. His behaviour that evening was, to say the least, verging on the outrageous though it seemed the chemistry between us was pretty good. I remember asking him to pick some of his favourite records of the moment and was astounded at his musical knowledge. It was like 'Trivia Freaks' night out! I vaguely remember the pop quiz which continued in a Manchester night-club until the very early hours. I also remember Elton being pretty upset at the absence of that hostelry's part-owner, one George Best!

That's our real problem – we're both football mad. Elton has commanded tremendous respect from everyone in football for the way he has conducted his dual responsibilities as Chairman of Watford and international pop star – at face value an almost impossible combination.

My respect for the man is immense. He is simply an exceptionally charming person with a quick wit, and a great musical talent.

My memories of the interview which follows are varied. I knew it was a mistake to be shown his record collection – quite the most remarkable I have ever seen! And I will admit to being somewhat disconcerted to find a Rembrandt adorning the wall in, as Elton John's Stateside fans might say, the John john!

Thank you Elton, for your time but most of all for being one of the great characters of British popular music.

ANDY PEEBLES

THE INTERVIEW

ANDY PEEBLES: Elton, firstly I want to extend grateful thanks to you for allowing us to enter your abode.

ELTON JOHN: That's quite all right. I hope you didn't get savaged too much by the poodles. (Laughs)

ANDY PEEBLES: Yes, the dogs. I suppose I ought to start by saying – as we're in your home – have you had much of a security problem since you've lived here because of the state of Elton John in 1980? I suppose you get harassment from fans . . .?

ELTON JOHN: Well no, really, the land mines tend to put them off, you know, and the sixty-eight-foot wall with the electric fence, you know, and the constant Dorothy Squires records blaring out of the loudspeakers, tend to drive people away. We don't actually get much trouble, no. We get people banging on the gate but no, not really.

ANDY PEEBLES: It's a lovely part of the world, though.

ELTON JOHN: It is.

ANDY PEEBLES: I want to go back to Pinner in Middlesex where you were born on 25 March 1947. And during the course of this Bank Holiday Monday afternoon, we shall have a look at your career and it's been very, very interesting. 1964 – just before we started the programme, we were chatting: you were playing with a band called Bluesology which I know, makes you a huge soul fan. You have been and you still are.

ELTON JOHN: Well, originally when we first started off as a semi-professional group, when I was working in Mills Music as a tea boy, packing up parcels and taking messages to Joe Loss, we thought we were a cut above the local sort of groups that were playing *Apache* and things like that still, and Beatles' songs. We played Jimmy Witherspoon numbers and any obscure blues things that we could find, which didn't give us a particularly big audience, but it did wonders to our own egos because nobody else did them. I mean, it was *Times Getting Tougher Than Tough* and a couple of Mose Allison things. Let's face it, I was just an organist and a pretty bad organist. All I had was a Vox Continental organ which I never repaired from the time I got it from the day I lent it to someone and never saw the next bit of it.

ANDY PEEBLES: You'd had a career playing with a band and you then went into a period where you obviously wanted to become a successful singer-songwriter, either with a new band or on your own. Was that a lonely experience to just have to sit down and start thinking of a solo career as such, having worked with other musicians?

ELTON JOHN: We were backing Long John Baldry as Bluesology when I left, and it was after he'd had hits like *Let the Heartaches Begin* and *Mexico*, and we went from playing sort of really nice places like the Rikki Tikk, Windsor and the Mojo Club, Sheffield into playing the Cavendish Club, Sheffield and sort of cabaret places and sort of having to set your equipment up during bingo sessions. The most insulting thing for a musician, if he's enjoying his work and really putting a lot into it, is to play to people that aren't interested in what he's playing. I always feel sorry for guys who play in piano bars when everyone's talking away, and sometimes if people are good pianists, nobody's even paying any attention. So being a meek little fellow in those days, I can never remember how I actually got the courage to actually say, I'm going to leave this band. But I didn't leave it abruptly. I was looking around for something else to do while I was still in the band. And I just answered an advertisement in the *New Musical Express* saying, 'Talent Wanted: apply Liberty Records'. So I did that while I was still in the band and when I got fixed up with a certain amount of income, I left the band and Jimmy Horowitz took my place. We used to play the Princess and Domino Clubs in Manchester and doubling gigs in the early days. I remember doing four gigs in one day when we backed Billy Stewart. We did the US Servicemen's Club in Lancaster Gate in the afternoon, nipped up (nipped in a Commer Van is not really the right expression!), 'nipped' up to Birmingham and played the Ritz and Plaza up there, and then came back and played the Cue Club in Praed Street in Paddington, London about six in the morning – setting up your own equipment.

ANDY PEEBLES: You talk about it very philosophically now, but I mean, are they happy memories?

ELTON JOHN: They're very happy memories, yes. I can't ever remember being miserable, even though when the van breaks down when you're on the road from Skegness to Boston at three-thirty in the morning, and it's snowing, it isn't particularly cheerful. I don't have any bad memories of it at all. When we first turned professional, Bluesology, the first person we backed was Major Lance. And then we backed Patti La Belle and the Bluebelles. Billy Stewart, who was an idol of mine, and died very shortly after he left us – went back to America. He was shot dead. One of the best examples, probably, would be a Billy Stewart record and *Sitting in the Park*. Georgie Fame in fact had a hit with it. And Billy Stewart was an enormous man. I mean, I remember stopping alongside the motorway on the M1, waiting for him to relieve himself, and it was like waiting for a train! So *Sitting in the Park* reminds me of Billy Stewart. He was tremendous.

ANDY PEEBLES: You're obviously a man who has memories firmly implanted in the old brain cells, and likes looking back on them from time to time.

ELTON JOHN: Well basically, what I am is – the modern expression of course is vinyl junkie – but I grew up as a kid, surrounded by records and I've always loved gramophone records and I think if you grow up like that and you're interested in records, you never lose that. And so to be actually backing people that I idolised and brought records from – like *Um Um Um Um Um Um* by Major Lance – there I was standing there playing it.

ANDY PEEBLES: So, having answered the advert that you mentioned a little earlier in our conversation, what breadth of time was there between answering that and let's say, the release of *Lady Samantha*, which I'd like to play, if it's okay with you? Which was what – January 1969?

ELTON JOHN: Well, a good deal of time, actually, because I went to Liberty Records which were an independent company in London. P. J. Proby was on their label; Idle Race made their first wonderful record with them.

ANDY PEEBLES: That was Jeff Lynne's first band wasn't it?

ELTON JOHN: Yes, *Climb Aboard My Roundabout*, [sic] great record. Anyway, I went up there and they said what can you do? And I said, well, I don't know really. I might be able to write melodies but I'm no good on lyrics. And they said, well, we've got this lyric writer, and gave me a lot of Bernie's stuff. This is Ray Williams actually, who did this. And I took it away and wrote some songs. In fact, I never met Bernie until about six or seven weeks at least, until I'd written some of the songs to his lyrics. And then he came down with this tatty little suitcase from Lincoln and we decided to try and make a go of it. First of all at Liberty I did a record test, because I thought I might be able to sing, and they said, right. You go into a studio, which was Regent Sound in Denmark Street – and sing. And the only song I ever sang was *He'll Have To Go* by Jim Reeves, which was years ago in the pub. It was the only song I could remember and it was so awful and they rejected me as a vocalist and Ray Williams then took me to Gralto – the Dick James Company, but actually it was the Hollies' company. Graham, Alan and Tony and I were signed to Gralto for the first few songs that I ever wrote with Bernie, and then, because it wasn't the Hollies' fault – they didn't know what was going on with their company – there were so many people in Dick James's studio doing demos. Dick one day had a massive clear-out and Caleb Quaye, who became very friendly, pleaded my case. He was working in the studio for Dick, and Dick signed us up to Dick James Music for £10 a week. And for two years, we tried to write songs for Lulu and Englebert Humperdinck. I actually got one into the last six of the Eurovision Song Contest, called *Can't Go On Living Without You*. I made a record called *I've Been Loving You*, which died the death. That . . . I credit it to Elton John/Bernie Taupin but it was all my lyrics, (Laughter) and actually the result of two years of depressing work and trying to get cover versions, it was really depressing. The only light came when Roger Cook and Roger Greenaway who were very helpful to us – Roger Cook recorded *Skyline Pigeon* and it got a lot of airplay – but really the first person to really motivate us at Dick James's was a guy called Lionel Conway and then Steve Brown, when he joined. I never had any aspirations at that point to become a vocalist at all. And I got pushed into making a record of *Lady Samantha*, which I hated, but Steve Brown liked, and it came out and it got a reasonable amount of airplay.

ANDY PEEBLES: What do you think about it eleven years on? I mean, do you still hate it? Do you still not like it?

ELTON JOHN: I always remember being absolutely horrified at the fact that the Wurlitzer piano that we hired for the session had a note out of tune and I couldn't play one of the notes that was essential and I hated it. I was very bigoted in those days.

And Steve Brown was a very wise man, and said go away and listen to it for two or three days and see what you think. And after two or three days I said, okay, release it. You know, can't do me any harm.

ANDY PEEBLES: Place your fingers in your ears and we'll play it. . . . *Lady Samantha*, from January 1969, and in the summer of that year there came the first album which was called *Empty Sky*. Does that bring back good memories to you now?

ELTON JOHN: Oh tremendous. I mean, this was at a time when records were real fun. I mean, it was the sort of the height of the flower power thing – the new super-groups: Crosby, Stills Nash and Young, and we had a couple of friends who ran Music Land Record Store in Berwick Street, which was one of the top import record shops, and we used to go down and help behind the counter and things.

ANDY PEEBLES: Yes, you used to work in there, didn't you? Somebody was saying.

ELTON JOHN: Well, not really work but . . . help out.

ANDY PEEBLES: Well, just go and help out.

ELTON JOHN: Ha! *C'est la vie*, but I remember standing there till nine o'clock at night trying to get the new Leonard Cohen album, and I know for a fact that the top-selling import album on catalogue was the Soft Machine album, which I don't think was ever released in England for years. And anyway, apart from trivia like that, *Empty Sky* was the first album we made. It was made at Dick James's studio, which was only like an 8-track, and I had a great time making it. It was when I first really used Dee Murray and Nigel Olsson. *Empty Sky* in fact, is still one of my favourite rock 'n' roll tracks. To get Caleb Quaye who was also very bigoted and only wanted to play like Jimi Hendrix, to try and get him to play like one of the Rolling Stones, we had to sort of coax him with Jimi Hendrix records and things like that. As far as a rock 'n' roll track, it still gives me great pleasure and the electric piano sound on *Sails*. Just little silly things that the public wouldn't notice, that when you make records you do, and for a studio that size it was quite a good little album.

ELTON JOHN: You can see my pathetic imitation of Mick Jagger on that record. I still like it, though, because it was a tribute. A lot of my records throughout my career have been misread as being trite, but really, some of them may have been, but some of them have been actually tributes to sort of heroes of mine.

ANDY PEEBLES: April 1970: the *Elton John* album, which is probably my first real musical recollection of Elton John as Elton John, it had a very striking cover, with all of you, I think, in a line on the back wearing fairly colourful clothes and the rest of the cover, I think I'm right in saying, was black, wasn't it?

ELTON JOHN: Yeah. It was, try and hide as much of his face as possible on the front, and it was a very moody cover. That moody cover fooled a lot of people actually, because Steve Brown stopped producing me. He said, I don't want the responsibility any more. He knew the songs. We had these songs in the can and he heard *Space Oddity* by David Bowie, which Gus Dudgeon had produced, and he made an appointment for Bernie and I, and himself, to see Gus and we played all the demos and songs to Gus and Gus wasn't exactly jumping over his seat with excitement. We planned that out and we had to because of budget. In those days that album cost about £5000 to make, which sounds ludicrous now but it was orchestral. All the things were planned. All the notes were written down, even the rhythm notes. I had to play live with everything. Can you imagine? I mean, they had all these brilliant session musicians standing there, the string players and I had to play live, and if I made a mistake that means they went. Oh God, it's back to looking at the newspapers again. It was a very, very disciplined album for me to make. A very enjoyable one and to Dick James's credit he invested a lot of money at that time, because it doesn't sound anything now, but albums are so ridiculous – gone over the top. *Border Song* came out and got me a lot of recognition as far as a lot of air play. I remember doing *Top of the Pops*. It was my first ever *Top of the Pops* with *Border Song*, and Dusty Springfield said she liked it and that made my year, because I'm a Dusty Springfield fan. And then, Dick said to me one day, they want you to go to the States, to Universal – it was Uni Records which is MCA – want you to go to America and appear at a showcase place called the Troubadour for three or four days, and they really think they can break your record. This was at a time when we started doing a lot of gigs and we were getting a good reputation as a live band in England. I did a disastrous festival in Crumlin in Halifax. There was so much squabbling about who was going to be top of the bill, I just said, Oh I'm going to go on now, and then after I went off, the heavens opened and that was it. And I got good reviews, and I didn't really want to go to America because I wanted to sort of maintain the reputation the band was getting over in England. And I sulked and became a prima donna a little bit in those days.

ANDY PEEBLES: You'd presumably never been to America?

ELTON JOHN: No. I wanted to go but I didn't think the time was right, because I thought, how the hell are they going to break a record by just playing a club for three days? The funniest thing was that Jeff Beck asked to join the band, you see. This is not a very well-known story, but it's true. And we played the Speakeasy Club in London and Jeff Beck came down. This was just after he'd had his accident and he hadn't been anywhere for two years and said, Can I join your band? And I was very adamant about no guitars, but it was Jeff Beck and I was little Elton John and I said, Well, we're rehearsing in Hampstead town hall, or something, come into rehearsals. They went tremendously well and I got very excited and then Jeff's manager came into Dick James's and said, Well, Jeff's very popular in America, (which he was) and he'll earn like, $15,000 a night, $10,000 a night. He'll take ninety and split ten per cent between the three others. And I was sitting there going, what? All that money, America, Jeff Beck? Wor, wor. And Dick sitting there going, in six months Elton John will be earning $25,000 a night himself. This is before the *Elton John* album came out. That was it. Jeff Beck couldn't join the group.

ANDY PEEBLES: Is he still a player you admire?

ELTON JOHN: Oh yes, very much. I mean, at the rehearsals we had, he fitted in perfectly. He was a fantastic guitarist and the ironical thing was in six months' time, I was earning more than that and Dick was right, but I mean it was only probably luck. So anyway, we went to America. We went and played the Troubadour Club in Los Angeles, which is only two hundred and fifty people. Everybody expected I think, us to come out with the symphony orchestra and me, because of the cover, to be terribly moody. And I came out in Mr Freedom clothes which, Mr Freedom clothes in those days were very adventurous and all my clothes were made by Mr Freedom. And I just jumped over the piano and we played rock 'n' roll mostly. And people just could not believe their ears or eyes, because there was no other group in the world that were playing rock 'n' roll with piano, bass and drums. Lee Michaels just had organ and drummer.

ANDY PEEBLES: Oh, I remember Lee Michaels, yes . . .

ELTON JOHN: And Emerson, Lake and Palmer were organ, bass and drums.

ANDY PEEBLES: But they weren't doing what you were?

ELTON JOHN: They weren't pianos, and people just went crazy and a guy called Robert Hilburn from the *Los Angeles Times* gave me the rave review of all time, and it spread across America and I became like an overnight sensation. It was incredible. I mean, it's luck. Right place, right time. Didn't want to go in the first place. Got talked into it. Sulked. And there I was and a phenomenon, literally overnight.

ANDY PEEBLES: Well, we'll get to that in a moment because I do want to play *Sixty Years On* from the *Elton John* album. It's always been a favourite of mine because the string arrangements absolutely fascinate me. Is this the track, you said you did all the tracks live, does this include this one?

ELTON JOHN: Yeah. Paul Buckmaster is a genius – revolutionised string playing with the *Elton John* album. I mean, people still up to this day come and say the production, the drum sound, the strings on that album. . . .

ANDY PEEBLES: Quite magnificent.

ELTON JOHN: Gus Dudgeon had phone calls in the night from producers. Buckmaster's contribution to the album was absolutely phenomenal.

ANDY PEEBLES: *Sixty Years On*, I regard that as a sort of miniature masterpiece. That sound really is quite extraordinary. It's nice to hear that again. An album with happy memories for you?

ELTON JOHN: Absolutely. As I say, terrifying to do, a privilege to work with such a big orchestra and someone as talented as Dudgeon and Buckmaster.

ANDY PEEBLES: We should at this stage, Elton, mention *Your Song* which is so often played on the radio. Do any of your records, because they get such extensive air play, even years afterwards, do you think, I wish people would play something else? And I'm as responsible for this as anybody else, but if I can cite *Your Song* as an example, I mean, that is probably one of the most played Elton John oldies, certainly in this country.

ELTON JOHN: Yes, I think people do tend to play the most famous ones. There are songs that I've written that I think are as good but don't get played which does sort of slightly annoy one. There's quite a few on each album that I regard as good songs. *Your Song* you just can't get away from. It is a beautiful song. It's lyrically beautiful. It was written in five minutes, recorded in two. (Laughs) The ironical thing was that the *Elton*

John album and *Your Song* were hits in England after they'd become hits in America.

ANDY PEEBLES: Talking about the relationship with writing with Bernie, because we dealt with that very briefly nearer the beginning of the programme – he was writing lyrics, you were writing music. That's a fairly unique concept, isn't it? I mean, was there any cross over? Was there any time Bernie ever sort of aspired to do a bit of music and forget the lyrics?

ELTON JOHN: No. Absolutely not. I mean Bernie's lyrics if you saw them, they're not iambic pentameter at its best. They're like seven lines, then three, then four, then nine, and I'd do a lot of crossing out, and we just clicked and it was just magic. Right place at the right time again. But I never interfered with lyrics, except I crossed out lines here and there, but he didn't interfere with melodies. It was just purely on that basis, although I knew what he was writing about most of the time, because we lived together at my parents' house. We were like brothers. So I knew exactly what he was getting at in *Your Song* and I knew in *Tiny Dancer*. It was very easy to interpret his songs.

ANDY PEEBLES: One of the things I'd like to do, Elton, is occasionally during the course of this programme, to get you to choose tracks which bring back memories of certain periods of time and if we go back to 1970, I think you mentioned you wanted to play *The Weight* by The Band?

ELTON JOHN: Yes. I remember listening to John Peel on the Sunday afternoon and he played this track and I stopped in my tracks, and I rushed down to Music Land on Monday morning and I just got about one of the last remaining copies. And that became a cult album at the same time maybe, as Delaney and Bonnie's album. I'm not quite sure. My memory's not that good. But *The Weight* by the Band is certainly one of my favourite all time . . .

ANDY PEEBLES: *The Weight* from the Band – a classic track which often comes up on my afternoon programme in listeners' all-time top tens. Elton you've, of course, done a programme for Radio One – I remember I heard it. EJ the DJ. You're very into broadcasting, actually, aren't you?

ELTON JOHN: Well, I like collecting records and listening to all sorts of records, and I've got a little DJ outfit at my house.

ANDY PEEBLES: Yes, I've been looking on your conducted tour of the premises.

ELTON JOHN: And if people come down and there's a disco, I always end up by just being the DJ for the night. You see, it all goes back to the childhood when I used to sort of watch the records go round on the 78s. I always remember the labels, you know, and they were all very dull except the MGM which was bright yellow and black. It's called vinyl in the blood, you know. I like being DJ because there's so many great records that people miss. There are a lot of good American records that English people don't pick up on. It works both ways. For example, *2,4,6,8* – Tom Robinson, or *Come Up and See Me*, Steve Harley, didn't sniff at all in America and you get things like, *We've Got Tonight* by Bob Seger and a couple of Steely Dan's things and Christopher Cross that don't even happen over here. It's . . .

ANDY PEEBLES: What do you think it is? Do you think it's a musical block somewhere between the British record-buying public and the American record-buying public, or is it just chance and fortune? The record doesn't have the right appeal? I think I've said this before on radio. I fail to comprehend how a record can get into the top five in America, and sometimes not even chart in this country. I mean that just seems very weird.

ELTON JOHN: I don't know. I really can't put my finger on it. People obviously don't like it. I mean, *Little Jeannie* for example is three in America and didn't do much over here. That's probably not fair because my singles have always done better in America than they have over here. But it is strange. I mean, a record like *You Light Up My Life* by Debbie Boone which was Number One for yonks.

ANDY PEEBLES: That's right.

ELTON JOHN: Which one would think if Lena Martell could be Number One, then a record like *You Light Up My Life* could be – thank God it wasn't, because I hated the thing. But I mean there are certain records which one crusades for. Andrew

Gold's first record that I was always playing – *The Way Love Is* or something like that.

ANDY PEEBLES: We go back now to *Tumbleweed Connection* which followed the *Elton John* album. Once again Gus Dudgeon produced the album. Was this a relationship which at the time, you hoped was going to last?

ELTON JOHN: Yes. The partnership it became, because I got on so well with Gus and Paul, and all the songs for *Tumbleweed* were more or less written at the same time as the songs for the *Elton John* album and the albums were recorded very, very close together. It was just that we split the songs up that were funkier really, for *Tumbleweed*. Gus didn't think Nigel and Dee were good enough to use on the record and I fought tooth and nail to get them on one track on the album. They're on *Amoreena* which is actually my favourite track on the whole album. That's my Van Morrison influence coming out there: *Astral Weeks*.

ANDY PEEBLES: It's interesting you mention the fact that the producer didn't like the musicians that you brought forward to play on the album, because, of course, just prior to that era there'd been quite a few interesting cases of bands – I always remember (I hate to mention it and they'll probably murder me for doing so) but the *Love Affair*. There was a huge kerfuffle over *Everlasting Love*, when I think Jonathan King, bless him, revealed to the nation that Clem Cattini had played drums on it and that all sorts of people . . .

ELTON JOHN: But that was going on for years . . .

ANDY PEEBLES: But very frustrating for the musician who's aspiring and trying to make it, obviously, to be knocked back. I remember Paul McCartney telling me last Bank Holiday after we'd done the programme, that when they first went to do the first Beatles' single, George Martin said, no way, Ringo Starr is not playing on this record. I mean this is astounding to learn, years later on, but very frustrating for the musicians.

ELTON JOHN: Yeah. I mean, I love my band and we really were playing well and for me it was frustrating and yet, I needed Gus's guidance as well, and we were on to a successful formula and I wasn't strong enough personality-wise to force my case. After *Tumbleweed*, I did a free radio concert for WABC-FM in New York which more or less started the concert scene on FM Radio in America, which is great. WABC is now WPLJ in New York and it went out from A & R studios. A hundred people in the studio and we recorded it just for our own pleasure. And because there were so many bootlegs at that time (bootlegging was very, very serious then as it is now) but bootleg albums were especially big, MCA panicked and wanted to put it out. So we put it out and I'm not ashamed of it, because it's a really good live album but it wasn't really a legitimate album. It wasn't planned. *The Friends* soundtrack album that came out for Paramount was something that Bernie and I agreed to do before we'd even made it really big with the *Elton John* album. The *Elton John* album had come out but it hadn't been successful, and we signed to do this soundtrack album for *Friends*.

ANDY PEEBLES: Described by somebody as a swift slide into mediocrity. Was that a cruel attack on it?

ELTON JOHN: Well, no. The film wasn't that great. Lewis Gilbert was the director. It was an exercise in mathematics. It was an exercise using Buckmaster, who was one of the most unreliable people in the world when it comes to, Is he going to turn up on time with the score? And it was like, oh God, oh God, my cat spilt milk all over it, and things like that and you'd think, oh no. But it was an exercise to write forty minutes of stuff for this piece of film. Bernie and I actually wrote all the songs for the film before we even saw it. It was an exercise which I wouldn't go through again but I – looking back – I'm glad we had the experience of doing. Paramount Records said we'll do the cover, we'll take care of everything because DJM had always, and always gave us the freedom to do our own covers and everything. They were great. Dick James has always been exceedingly fair to me and I've been exceedingly lucky in the fact that I always have had freedom. I must stand up for Dick about this. Dick's been run down by so many people. Sometimes he didn't understand what we were trying to do, but he didn't stand in our way, and he supported us a tremendous amount and I was very lucky to have the freedom to choose my album covers. But Paramount came out with the worst album cover probably, I've ever seen. It looked like a Barbara Cartland dress. It was extremely pink.

ANDY PEEBLES: Pink and white . . .

ELTON JOHN: Pink and white . . .

ANDY PEEBLES: Bit of black and . . .

ELTON JOHN: It actually led to the ruination of Paramount Records in America, because to get a gold album in the States you have to get 500,000 copies sold. Well, I was riding on the crest of a wave at that particular time, and Paramount thought, ay, ay, we're not doing particularly well – all they had was *Wandering Star* by Lee Marvin – and we'll dump this album out and make a fortune. So they issued about 600,000 copies. Little did they know that they were going to get 599,000 of them back.

ANDY PEEBLES: I'd like to play *Michelle's Song* because I've always regarded that as a very nice piece of music.

ELTON JOHN: Yeah, I like . . . I mean, we tried to write the music as sympathetic to the script as possible. I don't think it's mediocre. We hadn't . . . if we were slipping into mediocrity then, we probably are into the sludge by now compared to . . . if that critic is still around.

ANDY PEEBLES: You mentioned a little earlier in the afternoon, Elton, your love of outrageous clothes and the fact that, very early in your career, you were looking hard at getting different things to wear on stage. You started at one stage, I think, to take it to the nth degree. I remember doing a concert with you in Manchester where you came on with the tallest top hat I think I've ever seen. It was covered in sparkles and all sorts of things. But I mean, what was the basic motivation behind the clothes on stage? Did you feel that that sort of presentation was lacking in this country, and that you could make it your forte?

ELTON JOHN: No. It was nothing pre-planned whatsoever. Again, analysing it, as a teenage boy I was never allowed to wear mod fashions, rocker fashions or anything. I wasn't particularly the right shape but had a pretty strict upbringing. When I was my own man at last, I just got carried away and had a good time. The most unfortunate, narrow-minded thing was that people said, 'He plays good music. Why does he have to do this?' And they wanted me to stay as little Elton John and dress sombrely like a Randy Newman. I wasn't like that. I was out to have a good time, bay*bee*!

ANDY PEEBLES: Have you found over the years, it's been a strain keeping up with the fashions? I mean, every time I see you, you're wearing a different outfit. You tend to go in colours. I mean, same outfits, different colours, I've noticed over the last few years on the few occasions we've bumped into each other.

ELTON JOHN: You see, everyone still expects me to wear glittery glasses and those huge high-heeled shoes. For example, when I first joined Watford, when I did the concert for them, I was six foot three and had pink hair. I am now five foot eight and have hardly any at all! People still say, 'Ooh, where are your glittery glasses?' In fact I haven't worn them for five years but that is the image that still goes round.

ANDY PEEBLES: Have you still got them though, because the collection must be worth a few bob?

ELTON JOHN: Yes, yes. They're still upstairs. But I did the Muppet Show and they made me get out some old costumes and I had the greatest fun doing that. I had to do *Don't Go Breaking My Heart* with Miss Piggy and those puppets are human. They are not like puppets. The people that work with them are brilliant and funny people. I had to do eleven takes before I could even stop laughing and at one point I broke down again and she just said, she looked at me and she said: 'I am not used to working with amateurs,' and stormed off and it was wonderful. I like to send myself up and she did it perfectly for me.

ANDY PEEBLES: I'd like to have been a fly on the wall, or maybe even a pig! *Madman Across the Water*, October 1971, said Elton John, 'I hate it.' But that wasn't totally the album that you hated was it?

ELTON JOHN: I didn't hate it at the time, no. On reflection the songs I like, the vocals I feel leave a lot to be desired. We had a lot of pressure making that album. Buckmaster, at that point in time, was spilling ink pots over the score with eighty string musicians sitting in the studio and it was nail-biting time. And it was also the end of the line, even though they weren't on much of the album, or any of the album, for Dee and Nigel. It was the time on stage where one felt that we had to expand and add, so when it came out, because of the other albums coming out so quickly – *11.7.70.* and *Tumbleweed* and *Friends* people said, Hallo, hang on a minute. There's been a . . . this is especially in America, this is ridiculous. He's had four albums out in six months and for the first time I had my first real bridge to cross. You always get bridges to cross in your career which is why you keep going, because it's nice to do that, but then I knew after that album that there had to be time for a change. I like the songs on the album. I don't like my vocal performance.

ANDY PEEBLES: Let's pick another Elton John favourite from some years ago – and Leon Russell, I think, comes up this time.

ELTON JOHN: Well, Leon Russell. When I first played the Troubadour the second night, Leon Russell was in the first row and you can't miss Leon Russell 'cause he's got that wonderful hair. And I froze because he was my idol at that time. And I toured with him a lot, second on the bill in the States when I first went there and I thought he's going to tie me up to a chair and beat me every night and say this is how to play the piano, you silly little boy. And in fact, he was the nicest guy to me and we jammed together and *Song For You* – if I ever had to write one song in my life, it would be *Song For You* by Leon Russell.

ANDY PEEBLES: *The Honky Château* album in May 1972 was recorded in France. In fact, you've just come back from France haven't you?

ELTON JOHN: I've just been on holiday, mate.

ANDY PEEBLES: You 'ave *une* affiliation *à* France?

ELTON JOHN: *Oui*! Well it's always been very lucky for me recording, but I actually only became popular there with the advent of *Blue Moves*, believe it or not. But I like recording in France, and I like France anyway, and I'd like to make a French record, sung in French, just for the French. I just get on with them very well even though they don't like our lamb! I don't mind. I mean, as I say, it was very successful. The *Château* was successful for us.

ANDY PEEBLES: I'm surprised that you haven't had greater success in France because . . .

ELTON JOHN: Well, I am now. I'm a biggy, now. A biggy. But it happened with the most unlikely album of all time – *Blue Moves*. Before that you couldn't give me away, and now because of that, my back catalogue's selling and everything like that.

ANDY PEEBLES: *Honky Château* was in fact the first Elton John album to go Number One in the United States of America. Now we know already from listening to what you've said so far in the programme, that you're a great chart watcher. I presume that was a nice accolade and something which must have thrilled you a lot?

ELTON JOHN: Yeah, it was tremendous. I remember exactly when it came out. I remember when *Rocket Man* was out in America. I can't remember which Rod Stewart record it was, but it was either *You Wear It Well* or *Maggie May*, because both of them were Number One hits in America and I was driving down Sunset Boulevard to a house I'd rented for the Summer at 'Malibu de bum bum', and there was this disc jockey on KHJ going, well, you know, that's Rod Stewart's new record and he really surely must be the Number One male vocalist around at the moment and er . . . then he said, Oh, I've had lots of phone calls saying that Elton John is. Well, I think Rod Stewart just about beats Elton John. And I'm sitting in the car fuming. And *Rocket Man* was the first . . . it didn't get to Number One I don't think. It got to Number Two, I think, in the States. That was the stepping stone. After the sort of crisis of the *Madman Across the Water* album, which wasn't really a crisis but it was a relief to know that the gamble had paid off. Davey Johnstone had joined the band; never played an electric guitar and suddenly the band was a whole different wave. This was a band on record now; no session musicians apart from Jean-Luc Ponty and people like that who were used on the album.

ANDY PEEBLES: *Rocket Man* was in fact Number Two in '72, at the time of the Apollo 16 mission. Was that planned or was that merely coincidental?

ELTON JOHN: No, it was purely coincidental. In fact I think the Kinks' *Supersonic Rocket Ship* was in the charts exactly the same time. That was the first big single I had in America. *Your Song* was big but *Rocket Man* was the first really big biggy.

ANDY PEEBLES: Round about this time, the name Hercules came into your life, didn't it, not only as a house but it was also an appendage to your name as it was then?

ELTON JOHN: Well, I changed my name to Elton Hercules John when I became Elton John. I didn't see any point in becoming Reg Dwight. In fact, I'm afraid that any letters I received that were addressed to Reg Dwight were immediately torn up. But you know, middle names are just so stupid, I just thought Herc . . . my mother said, 'Oh! Bloody Steptoe's horse that is.' So Hercules seems to me a sort of stupid name . . . you know. It was one of those silly choices that one has. At the time I used to check myself into hotels as HP Sauce and things.

ANDY PEEBLES: Elton, before we go any further, do you think we could possibly play something by Rod Stewart or would that offend you?

ELTON JOHN: No, of course not. Rod and I have got this wonderful reputation of being Phyllis and Sharon and that we hate each other, in fact we don't hate each other, it's like Bing Crosby or Jack Benny or something like that. I'd love to play something of Rod Stewart's – *You Wear It Well*.

ANDY PEEBLES: Do you see much of him?

ELTON JOHN: I flew over for his wedding anniversary this year. I like Alana, his wife, very much. I like Rod very much. I love his little girl. He hasn't had many friends in the business and actually, nor do I, I don't particularly want to stay up till four or five in the morning playing twelve-bar blues and going, Yeah, man. And that is reflected on a lot of albums I've heard recently. It sounds as if that's exactly what happened. Tough – there are a few songs that seem to go on and on – it sounds like coked-out music to me and I've been through positions like that, seen musicians get into that sort of situation. Rod and I send each other up sky-high, we're totally different and yet we're best of friends. And we've both had our goes at each other in the past but really we're very loyal, I'd give anything for him.

ANDY PEEBLES: Well, that's good to know. *Don't Shoot Me, I'm Only the Piano Player*, January 1973, Number One both here and in America and a great deal of success.

ELTON JOHN: Hm. I remember it coming in at Number One. We were in Jamaica trying to record the *Goodbye, Yellow Brick Road* album, it's – me and my bright ideas. Well, we've done two albums at the Château, let's go – the *Goat's Head Soup* album by the Stones had just come out – let's go to Jamaica. So we go to Jamaica, we land the day after the Forman-Frazier fight so the island is swarming, we can't get into a hotel, the band – sensible lot – they went off to the other side of the island, Ocho Rios, which is the more glamorous side. I'm stuck in Kingston in the Pink Flamingo Hotel, my only contact being just a room with an electric piano in it and I wrote all the twenty-one songs for the *Yellow Brick Road* in two days while the band – and I wouldn't go out my room, I was so frightened. It's a heavy place to go, Kingston. Les McCann actually was a saving grace, he was playing jazz in the hotel where I was staying, so I used to go and see him every night. Got to the studio, and the studio equipment wasn't up to par, and we got our own equipment impounded, it was a nightmare. And all the band were down having dinner and all the rooms are fairly open, it's an open hotel, and they were celebrating the fact that we were Number One and I was sulking because we were getting nowhere in the studio fast, but fast, and they heard this sudden shriek, this centipede about fourteen feet long had crawled over me in this room and I rushed down into the dining-room with just a sheet covering me. That – I always remember that as the *Don't Shoot Me* period and eventually we didn't record the album there in Jamaica. We went back to the Château and recorded it there. It was one of my – one of the minutes – 'We'll go to Jamaica' – and we went to Jamaica, it was a natural disaster except for the fact that I wrote the twenty-one songs there in two days.

ANDY PEEBLES: Well we'll come to *Goodbye, Yellow Brick Road* in a moment, let's play two of your favourite tracks:

Daniel and also *I'm Gonna Be A Teenage Idol.*

ELTON JOHN: Yes, now that was written by Bernie about Marc Bolan who was a dear friend of mine. At that time I used to live in the house called Hercules which was in Virginia Water. He used to come down with his ex-wife June. He would come down and tell me stories and say the record's done forty-five million today – he would always over-exaggerate but not in a flash way and – great little guy, never meant anybody any harm, and we wrote that song about him because that's what he wanted to be, and he was living his part to the full and enjoying it and meant no harm to anybody. Great tragedy that he's gone, because he was one of the few people that would come out with the most outrageous statements, I mean, and you could easily see it was Marc, it was like he was from another planet but with not a bad bone in his body and it's very rare that you find that amongst people.

ANDY PEEBLES: Let's move now to an album which a few years ago, Elton, when I interviewed you, you said at the time you felt was regarded by too many people, particularly in the Press, as being the high point of your career. Do you still see *Goodbye Yellow Brick Road*, the double album, as being a high in the career of Elton John?

ELTON JOHN: It was a high in the sense that it was a double album that succeeded. It was my first double album and it's very rare that a double album succeeds. It had a lot of hits on it. It had three hits in America, it had *Saturday Night*, it had *Goodbye Yellow Brick Road*, *Benny and the Jets* and over here the same too, but *Candle in the Wind* substituted for *Benny and the Jets* which was a hit later. We could have taken singles off of that album for years to come, but I didn't want to do that because I don't like scraping too many singles off too many albums. It is a good double album, but people regard that as the high point of my career because that was when I reached the first peak, you know, to have two Number One singles from that album in America – and for *Benny and the Jets* to be my first single to ever go in the R & B charts. The funny story being that I wanted *Candle in the Wind* to be the first single off the album and I was recording *Caribou* at the time, it was when we were in Colorado and I still to this day can't see *Benny and the Jets* as a hit single, but the guy called Pat Pipolo from MCA Records rang me up and said, You're Number One Black in Detroit, and I said, I beg your pardon? and he said, It's the Number One Black record in Detroit. I said, Black record – me in the R & B charts? Spit it out! (Laughs) Be it on your own head if it isn't a hit, you know, like really considerate of me. And it was really Number One R & B single, and the fact that the Detroit Pistons basketball team use it as their theme song – Detroit made that record for me. I've had a few R & B hits since and it's nice and as I say, sometimes an artist doesn't know what's good and what's bad, he knows what he feels about a track, but he doesn't know how to pick singles. As a high point in my career as a musician, I would probably say no, although it has got some nice things in it that I really like. There was a re-recording of a song called *Grey Seal* for example. . .

ANDY PEEBLES: Yes, I'd like to play that, if we may, in just a moment.

ELTON JOHN: Yes.

ANDY PEEBLES: Why a re-recording? How old was that song?

ELTON JOHN: Well, *Grey Seal* was one of the songs that was done on the *Elton John* album and wasn't good enough. In fact, I think it was a B-side on one of the singles and then I've always thought that the version that we did on the *Elton John* album wasn't very good and so I re-recorded it. I also did that with *Skyline Pigeon* as well and that was used for a B-side with *Lady Samantha*, an album that DJM re-issued. It was a very long cassette first and they withdrew it and then they put an album out of old B-sides and *Grey Seal* was originally done for *Elton John* and we re-recorded it for the *Yellow Brick Road* album.

ANDY PEEBLES: *Grey Seal*, there's *Funeral for a Friend*, there's *Love Lies Bleeding* – they've become classic songs in the Elton John repertoire – how many of them do you still do live? Or will you contemplate doing?

ELTON JOHN: Well I'm going on the road fairly soon. Last year I did a solo tour with Ray Cooper and I wrote a list down of all the songs I'd like to do, songs that aren't so well known like *Ticking* and *Come Down in Time* – it's very hard because you have to do a certain percentage of the things that people like, although I've taken risks in my career. I remember doing the whole of the *Madman Across the Water* album at Crystal Palace in the open air and dying a death, and people said, My God, why did he do that? I've always taken risks like that, and I did it at Wembley as well, when the Beach Boys were on, and the Eagles and I came on and played the *Captain Fantastic* album. One has to do that because otherwise one would come on still playing *Yellow Brick Road* all the time. There are certain favourites, like *Rocket Man*, I still like to play. . . .

ANDY PEEBLES: Yeah. It's like somebody turning round to you and saying, Come on Elton . . . Or turning round to me and saying, Please will you pick your twenty favourite records. As time goes on and as the roster of songs gets bigger and bigger, the problem I would imagine becomes insurmountable.

ELTON JOHN: Well, it nearly is insurmountable, but you usually get round it in the end. Last year I did *Don't Let the Sun Go Down On Me* instead of *Someone Saved My Life Tonight*. Next year I'll do *Someone Saved My Life Tonight* instead of *Don't Let the Sun Go Down On Me*. I always like to do someone else's song in my set. Last year I did *He'll Have To Go*, the Jim Reeves song which wasn't written by Jim Reeves, but Jim Reeves made it famous. This year I'm going to do a Motown thing – I think I'm going to do *What Becomes of the Broken-Hearted*?

ANDY PEEBLES: As a lover of songs, does there ever come a time when you're planning a tour when you think, I'd love to do that song? I'm talking about songs which obviously you didn't write, I mean is there a temptation ever to include one or two odds and ends that you like?

ELTON JOHN: I always try and do one now on every tour that I like. *What Becomes of the Broken-Hearted*'s a great song. *Blowing Away* by Bonnie Raitt – well it's not a Bonnie Raitt song it's by Eric Kaz.

ANDY PEEBLES: Just going back to your record collection which I've had a look at – it makes the BBC's record collection look interesting! I can't draw a parallel – but having said that, how much time do you actually spend listening to those records? Are they a collection of records which obviously you want to hold on to for posterity, or do you derive great pleasure from them?

ELTON JOHN: I play my records all the time – I get terribly upset now because in the old days, I'm talking even about ten years ago, you only had a certain amount of albums released every week. Nowadays it's ridiculous. Cassettes I take with me on my portable cassette system. File – I like to file my own records. I've never let anybody borrow them – it's a trait that goes back to my childhood – I won't let anybody borrow me records in case they scratch 'em.

ANDY PEEBLES: *Caribou* from June 1974 meant the arrival of Ray Cooper who has become such a character on stage with you . . . and a great player, I mean a great percussionist.

ELTON JOHN: Well yes, Ray's one of the most incredible percussionists in the world. He never was so wild with the band when he first started, but his whole character is, and it's because Ray was an actor at one point and was at RADA, and he added another dimension to the band and took a little of the emphasis off of me, and especially last year, and I've said it before, the only person that I could have ever done it with last year as far as going on tour, is Ray because it became a theatrical show. Ray had a lot to do with the planning of the show and a lot to do with the ideas behind it. He's not going to be in the new band. I want him to, he doesn't want to be there.

ANDY PEEBLES: Are you sad about that?

ELTON JOHN: Am I sad about it? Yes I am, and no, I'm not, because I think for the time being he and I should go our separate ways, but I'm sure we'll work again. I adore the man. He's taught me such a lot, not musically, he's been educating me a lot. He's an educated man. I love him very dearly. He's brought me through a lot of crises.

ANDY PEEBLES: But he has a tremendous following, doesn't he? I mean I notice . . .

ELTON JOHN: Yes, the concerts . . .

ANDY PEEBLES: . . . you know, 'Ray Cooper rules OK' T-shirts . . .

ELTON JOHN: . . . appreciation. He deserves his following – tremendous musician and he's actually just been doing a film, the Robert Altman film of *Popeye*, that's why he's not on the *21 at 33* album, if any of the fans want to know . . .

ANDY PEEBLES: Well that's interesting.

ELTON JOHN: . . . because Ray wasn't available at the time, which is a shame but he has a special place in my heart and I think – you know – there are times when you feel the time is right not to do things together, and I'm sure that Ray and I will work together again.

ANDY PEEBLES: Let us play *Don't Let the Sun Go Down On Me* from *Caribou*, if that's all right with you. Is that one of your favourites from the repertoire?

ELTON JOHN: I remember playing it to Rod Stewart. I was driving Rod Stewart into town from here, this house, once in a very fast car and he was absolutely petrified and I said, Oh here's my new single. So he said, Stick it on then. After half a minute he said, Slow one is it? (Laughter)

ANDY PEEBLES: Oh, what a wonderful quote!

ELTON JOHN: He's always been very critical of my records anyway.

ANDY PEEBLES: Well we'll play it for Rod then. . . . Elton, I think I'm right in saying that around about this time you signed an eight million dollar contract with MCA in America. Do figures frighten you in the business? Does money frighten you?

ELTON JOHN: It didn't in those days. I mean I was overwhelmed with the fact – I couldn't believe the amount of money involved but I've never actually thought about having a lot of money, and now I've earnt an enormous amount of money, but I've never become obsessed with it. I remember when it changed the face of the record business in a way. It made the record business more vulgar and I was partly responsible for that because I remember MCA took out a full-page advertisement in the *New York Times* and *Los Angeles Times* saying, We are proud to announce the signing etcetera . . . which was the start of the multi-million deal. I was lucky, you see. In all those years that the Beatles and Stones made records, and they sold countless records, they were getting next to nothing as royalties. I came along, benefited out of the knowledge that they didn't get anything and with good

CAMERA PRESS

Elton John in 1978, photographed by Norman Parkinson

Elton: the piano-player

TERRY O'NEILL, CAMERA PRESS

Above: The Elton John Band Tour, 1974. Elton with Bernie Taupin and a crew of friends. Below: Elton on his Russian Tour in 1979

GRAHAM WOOD, *DAILY MAIL*

Elton in his vintage Jaguar in the grounds of his country home. Inset: On holiday in Barbados, 1976

DAVID NUTTER

TERRY O'NEILL, CAMERA PRESS

ATV

On the Muppet Show with Miss Piggy and friends

ATV

BRIAN ARIS

At Woodside with Clarence Bunny

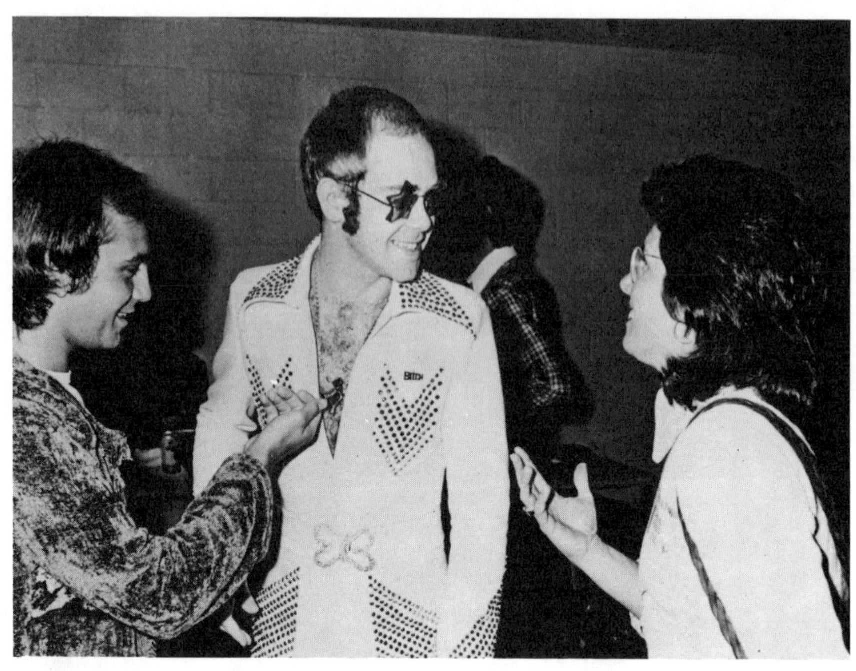

Above: With Bernie Taupin and Billie-Jean King. Below: With Queen

DAVID NUTTER

Above: With Kiki Dee, 1978. Below: Recording *A Single Man* with Graham Taylor, the Watford Football Club and Rocket Records staff, 1978

GAVIN COCHRANE

With the band, 1979: Kenny Passarelli, Roger Pope, James Newton-Howard, Ray Cooper, Caleb Quaye and Davey Johnstone

Above left: John Reid.
Above right: Gary Osborne
Bottom left: Bernie Taupin
Bottom right: With Ray Cooper
before his 1979 tour at Woodside

CHALKIE DAVIS

Insert left: 1979 – the first photo after Elton's hair transplant
Insert right: Andy Peebles

JOHNNY BEERLING

Elton John in 1979, photographed by David Bailey

management and good advice, benefited from everybody else's mistakes and came again in the right time, so I was very lucky in that.

ANDY PEEBLES: Which stage of your career do we find the name John Reid cropping up – with the name 'manager' in brackets after it?

ELTON JOHN: I met John Reid actually when he was working for Tamla Motown as a label manager at EMI in 1970. In fact it was John Reid who pulled *Tears of a Clown* off the Smokey Robinson album, made it a Number One hit, which was one of the first Number One hits Motown had had in England, which is very strange, but I think it was. I wanted him to be my manager, and he said no, because he wanted to stay with Motown, then I finally convinced him and I was being managed by Dick James at that time and John was managing me under Dick's guidance, then when my management contract ran out with Dick, John took over full-time.

ANDY PEEBLES: April and May 1974, I read, 'total exhaustion and fifteen dates cancelled'.

ELTON JOHN: Can't remember it.

ANDY PEEBLES: Really?

ELTON JOHN: No – no idea.

ANDY PEEBLES: 'A healthy man.'

ELTON JOHN: I can't remember that.

ANDY PEEBLES: 'Relaxed playing tennis with Billy Jean King'.

ELTON JOHN: Oh course, I did darling. (American Accent) Um . . . probably, I'm a big tennis fanatic and that's probably what I did. I can't remember actually. I've done so many things, I can't really put things into years. I really don't know.

ANDY PEEBLES: Let's talk about Rocket Records which is, nowadays, very much part of your life and I know means a great deal to you and probably means a great deal to the artists with whom you have worked. How do you see it in 1980, Elton? Are you happy with the sort of roster of talent that you have with Rocket? What's missing? What is there too much of?

ELTON JOHN: Well to start with, we all decided to form a record company about the time of *Honky Château* – us being Gus Dudgeon my producer, Steve Brown from DJM Records,

John Reid my manager, Bernie Taupin and myself. Let's form a record company. We'll sign new talent or talent that hasn't been given its proper vehicle and give them a good royalty to start with – eight or nine per cent to start with – which other companies wouldn't offer and also, because I am a record fanatic, a company that wouldn't be a vehicle for me. Like Swansong really was a vehicle for Zeppelin and Bad Company, Rolling Stones Records was Rolling Stones and the odd Peter Tosh record – I wanted mine to be a company that was started without me being involved as far as appearing on it. And we had a period of success with Kiki with *Amoureuse*, in the States we had Neil Sedaka with Cliff Richard and Kiki. The trouble is, within the record company, until the last year or so – it started out being too idealistic, too many friends were involved, I became too close. The decisions were never really made without everybody being involved, and it's a wonder that all the people involved that have worked for us and we still are friendly with, actually ever stayed – and it's great to be idealistic. It's like the Bangladesh concerts – what a great idea, but where does the money go? And as far as the artists go, we signed some pretty mediocre artists, we've had some good artists, we haven't done well by some artists, they haven't done well for us.

I think the situation nearly collapsed about two years ago when Gus left the company and Clive Franks and I co-produced Kiki and groups called China and Blue. I just got fed up with it. I like producing, but I was in the studio all throughout the year, and I gradually became more detached and John Reid wanted to become more detached and the people now in 1980, I'm talking about the English side of the company, are the people that have come through – like secretaries, Sally Atkins, John Hall, David Croker – who had a lot to do with bringing Judie Tzuke to the label – has now left and is working for another company. But it's mostly the people that have been there, loyal bunch of people, that are now running the record company and making decisions for themselves and that's the reason why I wanted a record company.

ANDY PEEBLES: Well *Greatest Hits Volume One* was

November 1974 and pretty well speaks for itself. *Captain Fantastic and the Brown Dirt Cowboy* you've already mentioned earlier on. I think I'm right in saying you performed the whole album, or nearly all of it, at Wembley on a gloriously . . .

ELTON JOHN: I played it all, yeah.

ANDY PEEBLES: . . . a gloriously sunny afternoon when my hay-fever nearly murdered the day for me. I remember that vividly. And the Beach Boys stole the show – is that a fair comment?

ELTON JOHN: The Beach Boys came on at a time when everybody was perfect. It was a beautiful day, it was six o'clock in the evening, people had had great music, they'd had Rufus, the Eagles, Joe Walsh . . .

ANDY PEEBLES: That's right.

ELTON JOHN: . . . I handpicked all the artists on the bill and at the time the Eagles weren't really happening, and the Beach Boys came on at the perfect time of day. We came on afterwards and played the whole of the album which, I mean, people don't like to go and sit at concerts, perhaps, and hear a whole album full of new stuff. I mean, I know when I go to a Joni Mitchell concert and she does some new songs, I think, oh go on, do one I know. But as artists, I thought I had to do it, it was a new band and as a new album, the previous band had made and recorded the album, the new band was playing it. I had to do it. Then we played the hit. The Beach Boys came at the right time of the day and they did probably steal the show, but we still went down very well.

ANDY PEEBLES: *Captain Fantastic and the Brown Dirt Cowboy* – was that a retrospective look at your career so far with Bernie Taupin?

ELTON JOHN: It was entirely about us, the whole album was written from my end on the SS *France* going from Southampton to New York, on the last sailing of the SS *France*. I tried to get the music room. An opera singer had it booked the whole time except for when she scoffed her lunch for two hours. So every two hours at lunchtime I used to go in there and nip out to the piano and wrote the whole of the *Captain Fantastic* album. First album that ever came into the charts, Number One in *Billboard*, which was a great excitement for me. That with *Rock of the Westies* following it was a pinnacle of sales. I mean that's as big as I got, to be honest. One couldn't really get any bigger than that, at that particular time. In fact John Lennon told me that at the time Jim Croce died, poor man, when his records started selling, you know, when you die your records sell, and his records were being played on the radio in New York all the time. John Lennon says, 'You're played enough', he said, 'if you ever die then I shall throw my radio out the window'. It was at a time where you couldn't switch a radio on in America without hearing one of my songs and, you know, people do get cheesed-off. I was cheesed-off with hearing myself as well, and that's why I started, instead of just doing albums, to try and do the occasional odd single. The single in America now is a bastardised form of selling an album and I wanted to put out separate singles just to prove that you could make five-and-a-half-minute singles that American AM radios would play and wouldn't edit.

ANDY PEEBLES: *Rock of the Westies* from October 1975 saw again a change in personnel, but some old names coming back with Roger Pope on drums and Caleb Quaye on guitar.

ELTON JOHN: Yeah, I couldn't believe Caleb had joined the band, he was playing with a guy called Bill Quaiteman in America at the time, and we'd still remained in touch and I'd never played with Caleb in a band before and always wanted to. It was the best band as far as musicians go, no as far as the whole sound – I'm not saying as musicians, that's unfair. But as a solid sound, the band – which I only had for a year between '75 and '76, we did two tours: *Rock of the Westies* and the *Rock of the Easties* – and after that I came off the road, but what a band that was.

ANDY PEEBLES: Kenny Passarelli?

ELTON JOHN: Kenny Passarelli with Joe Walsh, James Newton-Howard. I was desperate – I wanted someone to play synthesisers and I got him at the last minute. Roger Pope I'd known for a long, long time from Hookfoot with Caleb. Davey Johnstone was one of the few surviving members with Ray.

ANDY PEEBLES: And the LP was Number One in America and in the United Kingdom. Anything you'd like to play from *Rock of The Westies*?

ELTON JOHN: I like *Island Girl* and I like *Robert Ford* but can we play something a little different like – that was my first rock and roll album, it was a rock and roll band, it was a fun band, and the *Rock of the Westies* album, after *Captain Fantastic*, was a very lighthearted sort of album, so I'd prefer to play something like *Billy Bones*.

ANDY PEEBLES: I ought to mention that you were involved with Ken Russell's movie as the Pinball Wizard – I remember that.

ELTON JOHN: Yes.

ANDY PEEBLES: Did you enjoy that?

ELTON JOHN: I did except I had to walk in those bloody great shoes, I've still got them. When Ken Russell says, Walk, you walk and if I'd have fallen over them, I'd have broken my leg.

ANDY PEEBLES: I was going to say, actually, it looked decidedly risky.

ELTON JOHN: It was great fun, even getting up at five o'clock in the morning and there's a great story behind that. They tried to cast *Tommy* for a long time and Rod Stewart rang me up one day, said, They wanted me to be the Pinball Wizard. I said, Don't touch it with a bargepole. So – so about a year later, Pete Townshend rang me up and said, Will you sing Pinball Wizard? and I said, All right – it's a great song and I can't really go wrong, and of course I did it and it was an amazing success, the film and the Pinball Wizard track and I don't think Rod's quite forgiven me for that 'cos I told him not to do it in the first place. (Laughter) 'Cos he did it on the Lou Reisner album, you see, the late Lou Reisner unfortunately. If I can, can I play a couple of things that influenced, you know, a record that I really liked?

ANDY PEEBLES: Yeah, please do, I mean this is the whole idea . . .

ELTON JOHN: I remember rehearsing, the new band was in Amsterdam, and apart from 10cc *I'm Not in Love* which I won't play because everyone knows it . . . That was a big record for me, but so was the James Taylor album *How Sweet it is To Be Loved By You* and an Al Green record, *Tired of Being Alone*.

ANDY PEEBLES: I want to talk to you now quite seriously about the fact that in 1976 you became the chairman of Watford Football Club. I know that you had a relation some moons ago who played professional soccer, I'm right in saying that, aren't I?

ELTON JOHN: Yes, yes he scored a goal in the cup final, his name was Roy Dwight. He played for Nottingham Forest, broke his leg, more or less finished his career. But he was a very, very good player – on the verge of being picked for England.

ANDY PEEBLES: Now I also know through friends that I've got in football, that a lot of people in football have had tremendous respect, and I don't wish to patronise you at this stage of the programme, have had tremendous respect for the way you've dealt with this. I remember talking to you some years ago, and saying, Elton, wouldn't it be easy with your money when you arrived at Watford to buy up every available player that was on the market? To go to some of the big names and say, Look I'm Elton John, I'm chairman of Watford, here's X-thousand pounds for signing on and playing for my club, you didn't do that, did you?

ELTON JOHN: No – when I became chairman I had to get rid of the existing manager and find the best manager and the best personnel to run the club. I tried to get Graham Taylor once before when he was at Lincoln City and he said, No. And then I waited for him to come back from holiday, and I phoned him on the Saturday night he arrived back from holiday. I said, It's me again, and you've got to realise this was the time I'd come off the road, I hadn't had to do anything like this, and I was petrified on the end of this phone. So he came down to meet me, there were rumours of him going to West Bromwich Albion. I sat here with his legal adviser, my legal adviser for eight hours. We got on very, very well immediately because he's only a couple of years older than I am, his musical taste is abysmal (Laughter). Sorry, Graham. No, I've educated him a bit. I paid a lot of money for him because he was recommended to me by everybody. I beat West Bromwich Albion for him then I got Bertie Mee and I had to do the self-same thing. The whole team has been involved, it's taught me a lesson. I've made some awful mistakes as chairman, sometimes I haven't worn the right clothes when I should have worn the right clothes.It's all a matter of me learning at being chairman, and Graham is very quick to point this out to me, he's a disciplinarian. Because of our success from the fourth to the second in so many seasons last year, in the second division, I didn't see us win a match in the league. I saw us win in the cup at Queen's Park Rangers, but that was the only game because I wasn't here and I won't be here for another two or three years. Well, I'll be touring, I'll be here, but I won't see as much as I want to. But my chairmanship is something that I want for my life – for life. I can't see myself divorcing myself from the football club and the music, because I suddenly realised I grew up and we wanted to extend the ground. We had to have council meetings, it made me realise that I may be Elton John pop star and a lot of people know who I am, but as soon as I step into the council chambers at Watford to try and get some ground, or to seek their advice on extending our ground, that they hold the power, I don't and that's when I . . . for the first time in my life became politically aware.

ANDY PEEBLES: You actually wanted to build a new ground for the club didn't you?

ELTON JOHN: Yes . . .

ANDY PEEBLES: . . . and had permission refused.

ELTON JOHN: I think they honestly thought that I was going to pay for a new stadium. They probably thought I eat pound notes for breakfast, and that I would finance the building of the stadium myself, which I suppose is slightly understandable, but the only way that we could move, and they did offer us a site, but they wouldn't let us build anything commercial on it. Certain firms wanted to build our stadium, just to have a store on the site, you see, and so now we've been stuck in the position where we're going to have to enlarge our ground which doesn't exactly help the residents of where we are now.

ANDY PEEBLES: Mmm, difficult situation. I'm very interested

to hear you make the quote about the clothes, and turning up wearing the wrong clothes for the right occasion.

ELTON JOHN: No, there's a couple of times I've let the club down. I set myself a very high standard when I became chairman. I let it slip a couple of times and I'm glad it has been pointed out to me and I've known myself that I've been wrong.

ANDY PEEBLES: What's the general reaction been though, Elton, from fellow chairmen? I mean you see, to me as a football fan and I'm sure to a great number of people listening this afternoon, and let's say for instance, you and Bob Lord at Burnley are so many miles apart and yet you're doing the same job. How have they dealt with you, how have they treated you? Like an upstart and a pop star who's trying to be clever and do the football thing or have they said to you, good for you and we've got total respect for what you do?

ELTON JOHN: Quite honestly, throughout football I would say most people have treated me with utmost kindness and they've been exceedingly generous and extremely polite and very, very kind. There have been a couple of isolated incidents which one expected when I went in and became chairman of the club. I mean, I'd been chairman of the club since '76 but I'd been involved with the club eight years now, and after the initial reaction it's all died down a bit, and I'm sure there's a lot of talk behind the back when one leaves, you know, the board room but I must admit, most clubs and especially the bigger clubs have treated us, whenever we've played them in cup games and whatever, treated me with utmost kindness and consideration.

ANDY PEEBLES: What about your relationship with the players? I mean, do they respect you as being the chairman of the club or are they all Elton John music fans?

ELTON JOHN: No, I don't think hardly any of them are Elton John music fans . . .

ANDY PEEBLES: . . . are they honest enough to admit that to you?

ELTON JOHN: Yes, I think so. I wouldn't . . . I'm very honest with them. You see, Graham Taylor is an absolute genius in the fact that he and I respect each other, we're very competitive with each other, but he won't let me get too near . . . there has to be discipline in the team. I like the players very much as people and I like their wives, I like their children, and especially a couple of them that I know very well. I would love to have the opportunity of going round to their house for a meal, or a drink, but I can't, as long as they're still with the club I can't, because the discipline, you know, other players would get jealous and everything like that.

ANDY PEEBLES: Very difficult situation.

ELTON JOHN: It is a difficult situation and people would say, Well it's your club, you can do what you like, but it's not the point. I make a point of trying to know every player's wife's name. We have an open day every year before the season, when every member of staff at Watford won't leave the grounds, the bloke at the turnstiles comes to my house with their wife and their kid, and the kids . . . about sixty kids in me pool and five-a-side pitch, and it's an important thing if we're gonna do the things that we're gonna do at Watford the right way, it's going to take quite a few years. We did the fourth to the second in two years and I'm sure people, because I'm associated with the club think well, last year we'd go up to first. It would have been a disaster area because there is so much work behind the scenes to be done at Watford. I'm determined our club will one day do it.

ANDY PEEBLES: Well, from business moves at Vicarage Road to *Blue Moves* and an album which was released in October 1976. The front cover of which is actually over my left shoulder at the moment. This behind me is the original Patrick Procktor painting is it not?

ELTON JOHN: Yeah, it's a Patrick Procktor painting I bought at an exhibition. . . .

ANDY PEEBLES: . . . get your *Blue Moves* album out now from your collection and look closely at it and you can visualise what we're talking about.

ELTON JOHN: He's one of my favourite English painters and I bought it . . . it's called *The Guardian Readers*. There was supposed to be a competition in *The Sun*. They wanted to do a competition to give away like, win fifty Elton John albums and go to Blackpool, or win a hundred Elton John albums and go to Blackpool (Laughter) but they wouldn't do it because they said there's no women in this painting, you see, and I didn't realise before until they said this, but in the painting they're actually all blokes, but it's a lovely painting.

ANDY PEEBLES: Who's perfect? I'd like to play *Sorry Seems to Be The Hardest Word*, it's a lovely song, is that one you're particularly proud of as you look back?

ELTON JOHN: Yeah, I like it, especially as Frank Sinatra sang it on the Albert Hall when I went, and I didn't know he was going to sing it, and I nearly died. I've met him before but then I went backstage to meet him and the last night he was on at the Albert Hall – this was about three or four years ago, and he introduced me from the front. He's someone I admire because he always credits the writer, the arranger, and he tries not just to do his old songs, he tries to do obscure things – as an artist he's remarkable. When he introduced me I had to stand up at the Albert Hall and take a bow. I get very embarrassed with situations like that. I always think, well, Frank Sinatra sang one of my songs and one of Bernie's songs.

ANDY PEEBLES: You had all sorts of session men on that album. Do you find that a lot of people get in touch and say, look I'd really like to come and play saxophone on the next album or is it you that always goes to them? . . . the Brecker Brothers, David Sanborn, some great players.

ELTON JOHN: Basically, if I want to use someone that I admire like the Brecker Brothers and David Sanborn I ask them, and they've always been really co-operative.

ANDY PEEBLES: Have you ever had a 'no' from anybody?

ELTON JOHN: Well, I did ask Ann Shelton to tap dance on. . . . (Laughter)

ANDY PEEBLES: . . . you haven't had a 'no' from anybody?

ELTON JOHN: I don't think so, no.

ANDY PEEBLES: You wanted to play *Chameleon* which you wrote for The Beach Boys.

ELTON JOHN: Well, there was a period when Bernie and I were very frustrated, because not a lot of our songs have really been covered by a lot of people, and if they have done, they've not been really originally covered. So we set out to sort of write songs for people, and The Beach Boys actually came to us and said, Write us a song, baby. When I write a song normally it takes me twenty minutes, half an hour, top wack and I'm finished, and that's the way I write. With *Chameleon* I spent six months on it and I finished it, I always remember in Honolulu, Hawaii. I rang Taupin up and said, I've done it, I've done it, I've finished it and it was for me, it was what The Beach Boys were all about, and they didn't like it . . .

ANDY PEEBLES: . . . which must have upset you a little?

ELTON JOHN: Not really, I mean, it's their prerogative to say no. It didn't upset me, they weren't nasty about it, they just said we can't use it, so I decided to record it myself and use Bruce Johnston doing the backing vocals. (Laughter) And if you listen to it you can see that it was engineered and crafted for The Beach Boys. It's a very Beach Boys song.

ANDY PEEBLES: The Beach Boys didn't record *Chameleon*, Elton John certainly did and there was a bit of Bruce Johnston in there.

ELTON JOHN: I liked that sort of Beach Boys style.

ANDY PEEBLES: Elton, at this stage of the afternoon, let me get you to pick another one of your favourite tracks, and I think the name Bonnie Raitt comes to mind.

ELTON JOHN: Bonnie Raitt is one of the top three vocalists, white women vocalists in the world, one of the nicest guitarists, certainly one of the nicest ladies, and one of the sexiest ladies that I've ever met. I love her to death and she's never really had a big album or a big hit, but she's made fantastic albums, doesn't mean to say that she isn't great, but I've often found some of the albums of mine that haven't sold as much as the others mean more to me than the more successful ones. This is a track written by a guy called Eric Kaz, and it's called *Blowing Away*.

ANDY PEEBLES: What about your health? Because there have been one or two lapses in health, and you haven't been very well on various occasions during the course of your career.

ELTON JOHN: I must take this up . . .

ANDY PEEBLES: . . . please do.

ELTON JOHN: . . . I can't remember ever missing a show.

ANDY PEEBLES: Oh, not missing a show, I don't mean that.

ELTON JOHN: I had this sort of heart attack scare about two years ago, which was just nervous exhaustion. I went into hospital and it's great. If any of you artists want to sell more records, just have a heart attack scare and go into hospital, because your sales go up immediately (Laughter). It's incredible, I went in there and I remember *Part Time Love* was out and it was doing three thousand a day. As soon as I went into hospital, it was doing twenty thousand, great for your record sales. That was just nervous exhaustion. Last year at the Amphitheatre in Los Angeles, all of us, including the road crew got this stomach bug and I collapsed on stage and was led backstage and was made to be ill and then came back and I was fine. No, I've always been pretty fit, I hate illnesses. I always pride myself on not being ill.

ANDY PEEBLES: Do you feel it coming on though, or is it something that just arrives? I mean, do you know when you start to feel under par?

ELTON JOHN: There was this very vicious piece written in the *Evening News* by John Blake last year, saying that I was going round the world mentally driving myself into bad health and virtual insanity. Trying to get my old popularity back, driving myself into the ground, and all my friends were worried because I was going to have a heart attack. I have to have a full medical before I take a world tour, but I'm perfectly fit, you know, I'm not a great raver. I actually died in Barbados and Belgium in 1978 and not on stage, and I died in New York last year, someone had an obituary saying I was killed. But I'm fine, I've always been in pretty good health. Not particularly mentally sometimes, in '75 I wasn't particularly good in mental health. I was very, very untogether as far as my own life was going, but as far as physical health, I've always been pretty good.

ANDY PEEBLES: Do you find it easy to detach your own private life from your world of stage appearances?

ELTON JOHN: . . . yeah, exactly, you see my great thing is if you're gonna be successful and you are going to be a star, mystique. I used to go to a lot of concerts and a lot of parties and things, but on the other hand, everyone knows everything about me and everyone knows nothing and that's the way I like to keep it.

ANDY PEEBLES: It's a very interesting statement isn't it?

ELTON JOHN: Well it's true, I mean, in the paper every day, and yet most of what you read is absolute crap. I've just gone through my Press clippings. I own a yacht, a helicopter, I've done this, I've done that. . . .

ANDY PEEBLES: I mean, coming back to that I remember the glorious night, well it was glorious for you, not certainly for a great number of Mancunians when your football team, thanks to Luther Blissett – wonderful performance – beat Manchester United in the Cup. There again I could also say that the Stretford End spent most of the evening singing, 'Elton John's a homosexual'. I mean, it's an interesting balance isn't it?

ELTON JOHN: Well, when I came off the road in 1976, I was very mentally tired, mentally fed up with myself as a person. I was very untogether, not untogether, but I was very unhappy. I had to decide if I could go on touring, and singing *Yellow Brick Road* for the rest of my life which I hated and I didn't want to do. I couldn't do anything for myself. I was a helpless young man and I became the chairman of the football club which meant I had to hire people, fire people, go to the bank, do things that normal people had to do and people like me should be able to do, and one becomes so detached you do lose sense of reality. How much a pint of milk costs, and how much a first class . . . it sounds ridiculous, but this is true, if I'd have come off the road and had nothing to go into, God knows what would have happened to me. But I had the football to plunge myself into, which I went in with full steam as if I was having a new band and of course I've taken insults. I'm not stupid, I know that a lot of people, you know, when you're sitting at West Bromwich Albion and they're singing, 'Elton John's a homosexual', twenty thousand people singing that and you're sitting round the directors' box going, Nice day (Laughter) nice plumage! I used to be a bad loser, it's been very good for my temperament, I can see both people's points of views. As a person it's helped me tremendously.

ANDY PEEBLES: *A Single Man*, October 1978 with a front cover which was done, what somewhere in the Berkshire area? Where there's a rather splendid stately home!

ELTON JOHN: It was me being lazy. Terry O'Neill is a great photographer, and a big friend of mine, and I was in a lazy mood and we just went up the road to Windsor Castle. And so many people think that's the house in which I live because it's a long drive Windsor Castle, and I said, Well no I'm just one step further down the road.

ANDY PEEBLES: Did you have to get Royal consent?

ELTON JOHN: No, it was terribly embarrassing because there were picnickers and everything, we had to get them out of the way. Terry O'Neill was like a used-car salesman, 'scuse me love, get out of the way. . . .

ANDY PEEBLES: You were done up in morning dress weren't you?

ELTON JOHN: It was just an overcoat, a pair of old judo trousers and black boots and very sinister. I looked like an undertaker . . .

ANDY PEEBLES: Yes, you did . . .

ELTON JOHN: . . . but *Single Man*, actually was an album that wasn't meant to be an album. In fact, I went into the studio and did a record of *Ego*, which was a song which was a couple of years old, that Bernie and I had written, and also a song called *Shine on Through* which Gary Osborne and I had written. And because I hadn't written for so long, I sort of got writer's diarrhoea as I call it, and suddenly I began to write melodies first – after all these years of writing lyrics, lyrics coming first and then melodies. And Gary was around and I had a few ideas for a certain line to the songs, and certain titles and we had great fun doing it. For example, it wasn't the song, but *Song For Guy* was written, recorded and finished on the same day and unfortunately the tragic thing about that was, when I called it *Song For Guy*, the next day because the young office messenger Guy Burchett, from Rocket Records was killed on that Sunday on a motor bike. I had no idea what to call the song; I knew it was a death song. I'm very good at writing death songs, and I like death music, I don't know why. I'm not a morbid person but I do like anything that can . . . *The Enigma Variations* for example, you've only got to start playing and I'm in floods of tears . . . (Sigh). The thing that crucified me most was that in America they said *Song For Guy* wouldn't be an instrumental hit, because *Music Box Dàncer* by Frank Mills was already in the charts . . .

ANDY PEEBLES: Oh, that was a very big record wasn't it?

ELTON JOHN: And they said there wasn't room for two instrumentals. They said, We'll put it out to please you, but we won't do anything for it.

ANDY PEEBLES: Elton, the *Single Man* album was produced by yourself and Clive Franks, who I think I'm right in saying, is your sound mixer when you appear live, is he not?

ELTON JOHN: Yes, Clive has been my sound mixer from about 1972.

ANDY PEEBLES: Right, the last time that I saw Clive was on a very hot, very, very humid night in Moscow. Now with the Olympics just over, it brings back some amazing memories of your live concerts on Radio One from the Rossya Hall in Moscow. When you look back on the Russian tour, look at the Olympics, and the things that have happened since, did you see that tour as being a great achievement in your career?

ELTON JOHN: After I came back, after it was all over and done with, yes. Because initially, last year when I set out to tour with Ray, it was only going to be a little European tour to get me back into the idea of thinking about if I could play the piano well again, and sing well. And I enjoyed it so much. I wanted to be like theatre, and it was a challenge for anybody, egotistically I said this, I want to go out there with just myself and then Ray and prove that I can do it on my own, and I can play soft numbers. I can play rock and roll. I wanted to be theatrical, I wanted beautiful lights etc and go to places that I'd never been to before. Funnily enough, you know, I'd never played in France before, I'd never played in Belgium before, I never played in Spain before, never played in Israel before, never played in Northern . . . I made a point of going to Northern Ireland and Southern Ireland and Russia was the last thing, and by that time we were all fairly tired and my parents were invited and it was very sort of protocol. It's very easy, actually to go over there. Harvey Goldsmith said, Shall we go to Russia? So I said sure.

ANDY PEEBLES: Harvey, I should say . . .

ELTON JOHN: . . . he's the promoter. And we wrote a letter, an official letter to the Russian people, and then we had a reply back in eight days, a very polite one saying, We'd love to have you, we'll come over and see the show, which they flew over to see the show in Oxford. They don't like people saying that they're going to go to Russia before they ask. They're very correct people, the Russians, anyway my parents were invited and we didn't know what to expect and as far as the buildings, the atmosphere, the concerts were spectacular, as far as the fact that I was absolutely petrified before I went on. The people that looked after us, you know, it was the initial joke, are the rooms bugged? for the first time and then it all wore off. I know we got the best treatment and the best food. The people were so warm. I remember crying my eyes on a train going from Leningrad to Moscow, the night train, and all these kids, hundreds of fans who followed us around everywhere throwing all their favourite things in the windows and they probably spent a fortune for on the black market, and Bob Hilburn of the *LA Times* and my mother and I just sat in the corner of the train just bawling our eyes out. The friendliest, warmest people. We spent ten days there. I had the most fantastic time, culturally as well, seeing the most beautiful things. I came back and the first questions that were asked were negative. At London Airport, What do you think of Communism? First typical English quote. How the hell do I know what to think of Communism in ten days? There was not one positive question. I was criticised, and probably, you know, I thought about this, about going onto the dissidents sort of situation, because of the Jewish situation over there and the way gay people are treated in Russia and the fact that I didn't know before we went that only five per cent of the tickets went on sale to the kids, the rest of them went to the privileged people.

ANDY PEEBLES: That obviously worried you, I'm sure.

ELTON JOHN: It did when I got over there, yes. And it's like I said before, if you're gonna do a song, or make a statement about a cause it's all very well to say okay, we'll do a concert for No Nukes. Great idea, you know, you believe in it, fantastic you should do that, but to follow it up with, then don't just do the concert and it's all over and done with, in ten minutes. Follow it up, get a committee together go and meet political people, that's the only way that people are ever going to take you seriously. Because when I became chairman of the football club and I went to council meetings, I got my respect from being a fairly intelligent person, and, of course, people are going to be suspicious of pop people, that's human nature. If I'd have said I'm not going to Russia unless you sell all the tickets to the kids, then they would have said, Go away, don't bother. Now forget the Afghanistan thing, if I'd have come back after the successful tour and it was, we had a fantastic time over there, they were delighted, if I said to them next time, hey how about a few more tickets for the kids, maybe they would have said, okay, yeah, that is what I would have loved to have happened in Russia. Unfortunately, of course, they invaded Afghanistan. As much as I'd love to go back to Russia, morally I couldn't. No one loves sport more than myself, sport and music go hand in hand, the fact that it's a great outlet of aggression, you don't exactly have to be good at anything to enjoy it. You don't have to be a good guitarist to enjoy just strumming a few chords. You don't have to be a good footballer to enjoy playing a game of football or hockey or whatever it is, but the people in Russia don't really know what's going on in the outside of the world. If all the people, all the athletes that were told to stay home stayed home, then the Russian people would have just had European bloc countries there and Zaïre and countries that are Communist held, would have gone what the hell is happening? And it's very easy for me to sit here saying it, 'cos I'm not an athlete, but that is the only way of getting through to those Russian people who are very proud, sweet, kind people. They're like people like you'd meet in the street here and they're very nice people.

They're not informed people, they don't know what's going on, but they're proud of their country and why shouldn't they be proud of their country? I definitely wouldn't go to Russia while they're in Afghanistan.

ANDY PEEBLES: Elton John in Moscow, Leningrad and Russia. Elton, your twentieth album. I don't know whether I've totally got that right numerically, but October 1979, *Victim Of Love*, which I think I can truthfully say didn't happen. It was produced by Pete Bellotte. Did you see it as a bit of indulgence on your behalf musically?

ELTON JOHN: Before we deal with that, can we deal with the Thom Bell sessions?

ANDY PEEBLES: Yes we can.

ELTON JOHN: I did some stuff with Thom Bell with whom I've always wanted to do separate singles and I always wanted to work with Thom Bell because of the Stylistics things. I am a soul music fan and The Detroit Spinners records and I did some stuff with him, in I think, '77 and I was delighted with the rhythm tracks. There was one song that Bernie and I wrote, and one song that Gary and I wrote, and there were four of his own songs – Bell and James who actually had hits in their own right. And I went to Seattle to record and it all went fantastically well, and then I heard the mixes and I shelved them for a year because it was too saccharine and then decided to put out a maxi single in England. It was very strange, because there was one record called *Are You Ready For Love?* which was actually the A-side over here, which I asked Thom to put the Detroit Spinners on doing some backing tracks for us and when his mix came through I only sang one verse and they did the whole lot . . . I couldn't believe it (Laughter). There they were, I thought well, I only asked them to do . . . so I left it and I remixed some tracks and that came out before. So that was an indulgence on my part, I suppose, wanting to work with somebody for a new experience and Thom Bell taught me a lot. He taught me to use my voice in a lower register because he said, I've noticed you sing a lot in high in *Yellow Brick Road* and things like that. *Someone Saved My Life Tonight*. Use your voice lower, like in *Your Song* and you've got a completely another register to your voice and I did, and *Mama Can't Buy Your Love* did very well in America. In fact, it wasn't an album but the Thom Bell sessions got to about number fifty on the *Billboard* album chart. Then last year while I was doing the English tour, Pete Bellotte who has been a friend of mine, when I played The Top Ten Club with Bluesology, years ago in Hamburg, he was in the other group on the bill and I became friendly with him and his wife, he married a German girl and we stayed in contact. Then I sort of didn't hear from him for three or four years until I picked up a Donna Summer record and I went, oh my God, and he came to the concert in Drury Lane and said, Would you fancy doing an album? You know, like a disco-type album, not just a disco, I want to do rock and roll type thing. I said sure, I'd love to, because I do like disco music if it's good. I like any sort of music if it's good. I said providing that you get German people to write the songs and you do all the musicians . . . I said I don't have to play on it, which is more fun for me and then I go to Germany and put the vocals on it, and sing how you want me to sing. So I was in Grasse last year, 1979, writing the songs for *21 at 33* and I flew to Munich for eight hours and did the vocals. And it came out at the time when disco was peaking, and it came out at a time when it looked as if I was jumping on the bandwagon, because Rod had a success with *D'Ya Think I'm Sexy*, The Rolling Stones had *Miss You* and they thought, hello here's another biggie trying for a success. It didn't do my career a lot of good. I don't regret doing it whatsoever. I wanted to make a record that people could dance to in Rochdale or somewhere like that, or anywhere without sort of taking the needle off. I can understand why it wasn't successful. I enjoyed it, it was self-indulgent, but in the next few years the people will have to expect more self-indulgent things from me to appear. *Victim Of Love* in America with the singles . . . the AM stations played it, the FM stations wouldn't play it until they found the Doobie Brothers sang on it, then they played it. I mean how, you know, typical. I'm not ashamed of it, I'm not going to hide that record in the cupboard. I'm going to do *Victim Of Love* on stage, but no, it didn't do my career a lot of good, (Laughs) but I don't regret it.

ANDY PEEBLES: You just mentioned your love of disco music, now a track which I played some weeks ago, thanks to a tip-off from you via friends, and all the rest of it, is a French record which I know you love particularly by a lady called Janic . . .?

ELTON JOHN: Janic Prevost, it's a record I heard driving out of town in St Tropez in a traffic jam and it just suddenly came on. It's the sound of the record and it just sent shivers up and down me spine even though it was sung in French. It's her first record, I love it. I would love it to be a hit in England. In French, probably it wouldn't be, maybe it would need an English translation, but it's got a special thing about it, I don't know what it is. It's sort of like a *Song For Guy* record, it has an ambience that you can't put your finger on, but there's something that sends a little shiver up your spine, did mine anyway, but who am I to say? But I think it's wonderful.

ANDY PEEBLES: Yes it really is rather excellent. Elton, we're up to date *21 at 33*, a lot of people, I think in the business have been quite elated about the songs on this, the combinations with Tom Robinson, *Sartorial Eloquence*, with Judie Tzuke on *Give Me The Love*, your current single, with Gary Osborne on *Little Jeannie* which has done exceptionally well for you, and once again, the combination back with Bernie Taupin. Can I just clarify that position, what happened when you and Bernie initially packed up writing, did the well run dry?

ELTON JOHN: It was never a packing up of writing, the thing was, when I made *Single Man* I was firmly ensconced in England and was fed up with America and Bernie was firmly ensconced in LA and didn't want to come to England. Of the two of us, you would never have thought that I would have stayed here and he'd have gone there, it would have been the reverse in the early days; but it's worked out this way and of course when *Single Man* came out with all the songs with Gary on it, people's tongues started to wag. Bernie and I always kept in touch, it was just a time when I've always encouraged him to write with everybody else and I like writing with people all the time now. He's just written his own album, I started to write with Judie Tzuke and Tom Robinson on this album and Gary, of course, and I've always encouraged Bernie to write with other people as well and he's writing with Rod Stewart for his album. There was never any feud, you know, it's the typical thing you read in the papers just because he lived in America and I had an album out and he had an album out with different people, the tongues started to wag, and it's all told . . . on *Two Rooms At The End Of The World* tells it all.

ANDY PEEBLES: Yeah. What would you like to play from *21 at 33* as we get towards the end of what for me has been a very enjoyable afternoon.

ELTON JOHN: Well, I'd like to include a Taupin track and *White Lady White Powder* which I got The Eagles to sing on eventually. When I wrote the song, I thought there's only going to be one group that can do the harmonies on this record and that's got to be The Eagles. And I waited till they finished their tour of America in February and they're big friends of mine from a long way back.

ANDY PEEBLES: Elton we're almost at the end of the programme. A lovely, lovely house you have here, does it sadden you that you have to spend so much time out of the country?

ELTON JOHN: A lot of people think that I have to sort of spent a lot of time out of the country and I can't live here because of the tax. It's nonsense, I live in my house, it's just in the last year, because of my tour, and now I'm forming a new band, I'll be touring again, but I live in this house, this is the only residence. . . . I have a house in Los Angeles which I'm trying to sell because I don't particularly want to live in Los Angeles any more. I never did live there in the first place it was just that I spent so much money at the Pink Palace, this is the Beverley Hills Hotel, it was more of an investment to buy a house, but England is my home. I wouldn't mind having a little place in France, somewhere down the south of France where I could go away and write in the winter. If I'd have become a tax exile I'd have become one way before now, because I don't have to worry about tax. Mrs Thatcher has slashed it to sixty per cent for me, even though I didn't vote for her.

ANDY PEEBLES: Before we play *Sartorial Eloquence*, firstly I ought to extend a great big thank you to you for your hospitality, but more importantly I really ought to ask on behalf of everyone listening, when are we going to see you again, appearing live in this country?

ELTON JOHN: Well, I'm off now, more or less to do rehearsal for three weeks but in a new band which will be Nigel Olsson and Dee Murray, the old band . . .

ANDY PEEBLES: Amazing.

ELTON JOHN: . . . Richie Zito on guitar who played all the acoustic guitar on *21 AT 33* and the electric guitar on *White Lady White Powder*, Tim Renwick on guitar who played all the guitar on *Single Man*, James Newton-Howard on electric keyboards and myself and that's going to be the band. We're going to play America, Japan, Australia, New Zealand. I'm going to write and record a classical album in January and February.

ANDY PEEBLES: Are you?

ELTON JOHN: Yes.

ANDY PEEBLES: When you say a classical album, what sort of material are you looking for?

ELTON JOHN: Well James Newton-Howard and I always wanted to do a classical type album. It's really music for a film but I can't say anything more; I'm going to write the music and they're going to . . . someone's going to use the music in the film. But it's an album that James and I have wanted to do, and we're going to do it in January and February.

ANDY PEEBLES: In other words you're keeping yourself very busy indeed.

ELTON JOHN: Yeah, but after ten years of doing what I've done and going through all the achievements and all the work and all the things that I've done, I've enjoyed it, thank God, there's so many people that haven't enjoyed it. I've been lucky, because I've got lucky and good people around me. I've been a stupid person at times, but with the football club getting me along the straight lines again as far as turning me into a decent human being, as far as getting myself together, all that old American rubbish, but growing up is the word I think.

ANDY PEEBLES: Well, from a Manchester City fan to the chairman of Watford, I wish you a good season.

ELTON JOHN: And you too, and to all the soccer clubs throughout this country.

ANDY PEEBLES: Many thanks to you Elton for your hospitality.

ELTON JOHN: Thank you. And to all my fans, thanks for their loyalty.